The Mating Flight of the Queen and Drones

THEY WORK
Honey Bees, Nature's Pollinators

Copyright © 2025 by June Smalls
Illustration copyright © 2025 by Yukari Mishima
All rights reserved

Published by Familius LLC, www. Familius.com
PO Box 1130, Sanger, CA 93657

Familius books are available at special discounts,
whether for bulk purchases for sales promotions, or for family or corporate use.
For more information, email orders@familius.com

Reproductions of this book in any manner, in whole or in part,
whithout writtenl permission of the publisher is prohibited.

Library of Congress Control Number: 2024947920

Print ISBN 9781641709651
Ebook ISBN 9798893965094
Printed in China
Edited by Brooke Jorden
Book and cover design by Carlos Guerrero

10 9 8 7 6 5 4 3 2 1
First Edition

THEY WORK
Honey Bees, Nature's Pollinators

by June Smalls

Illustrated by Yukari Mishima

She is the queen.
She fought for that position from the moment she broke out of her cell.
Her job is important, but she is not the leader.

A queen is created by the hive when a new one is needed. They are larva that are fed a special diet of royal jelly. Worker bees secrete royal jelly from a gland on their head. All larvae get this treat for a few days, but only queens dine on royal jelly their whole life long.

When she is born, she'll fight other potential queens for her place. Once she is the undisputed queen, she'll spend her life laying eggs. She can lay up to 2000 eggs in a day, one egg in each cell.

Drone

A hive can have 25,000 to 100,000 bees depending on the time of year. A few hundred of them are male bees, called drones. They are dependent on the females and their only job is to sire the offspring. All the rest are females known as worker bees. They must work with little or no direction.

From the moment they push out of the cell where they grew as larvae, they have a job to do. In fact, they have all the jobs to do.

Each bee starts as an egg, smaller than a grain of rice. After about three days, they hatch into a fast-growing grub called a larvae. The larva becomes a pupa and then finishes their metamorphosis, emerging as an adult bee.

Each bee, newly free, dries off and eats their fill.
Now it is time for work. First as janitors, cleaning the cells of the nursery.

Female bees have to work their way out of their cell all alone, though workers help the male drones escape their cell and feed them.

Newly hatched worker bees clean the cells and surrounding area so it is ready for the next egg.

Then they are nannies, caring for the larvae.

Caring for hundreds of eggs and larvae takes a lot of work. These nurses feed the larva royal jelly for about three days before switching them to a diet of pollen mixed with honey, sometimes called bee bread.

Then they are the queen's ladies in waiting.

A queen is so busy laying eggs, she cannot groom herself, stop for bathroom breaks, or feed herself. Her attendants take care of her every need so she can continue the job of producing more bees for the hive.

Then they are construction workers and engineers.

Bees secrete wax from their abdomen. They use this wax to build comb on both sides of a base. Efficient engineers, bees create hexagon cells which give the best strength and storage area with the least amount of wax needed.

Then they work the kitchens, ensuring every bee in the hive won't go hungry.

Honey is created when foraging bees gather nectar from flowers. It is stored in a honey sac inside their body. Once back at the hive, they bring up the nectar into their mouth and bees in the hive take it from their mouth. Then they put it in a cell. It takes a few days to thicken into honey. The bees then put a wax lid on the cells.

Workers pack the pollen in separate cells.

Then they stand as sentinels.

Bees stand guard at the opening of the hive. They guard against attacking insects, like wasps, and thieving animals from moths to bears. If the hive is attacked, they'll give off a scent that alerts the other bees. Bees will give their lives to protect the hive, stinging the intruders.

Then they soar into the sky to forage for food.

Once they are old enough to forage, the bees fly around their hive to orient themselves. Then they'll fly for miles, gathering nectar from flowers.

Their hairy bodies, and even hairy eyes, gather pollen. They use comb-like hairs to brush it into sacs on their legs. The pollen trapped on their body pollenates the next flower they land on. This pollination is how a flower becomes a fruit. Humans rely on pollination for one third of our food.

Foraging is dangerous work.

Storms can wet their wings, predators hunt them, and pesticides from humans can poison them. But honeybees will forage until they are too old and worn out to forage any more.

They are even map makers, dancing a sophisticated dance in the dark of the hive, to show their sisters where to fly.

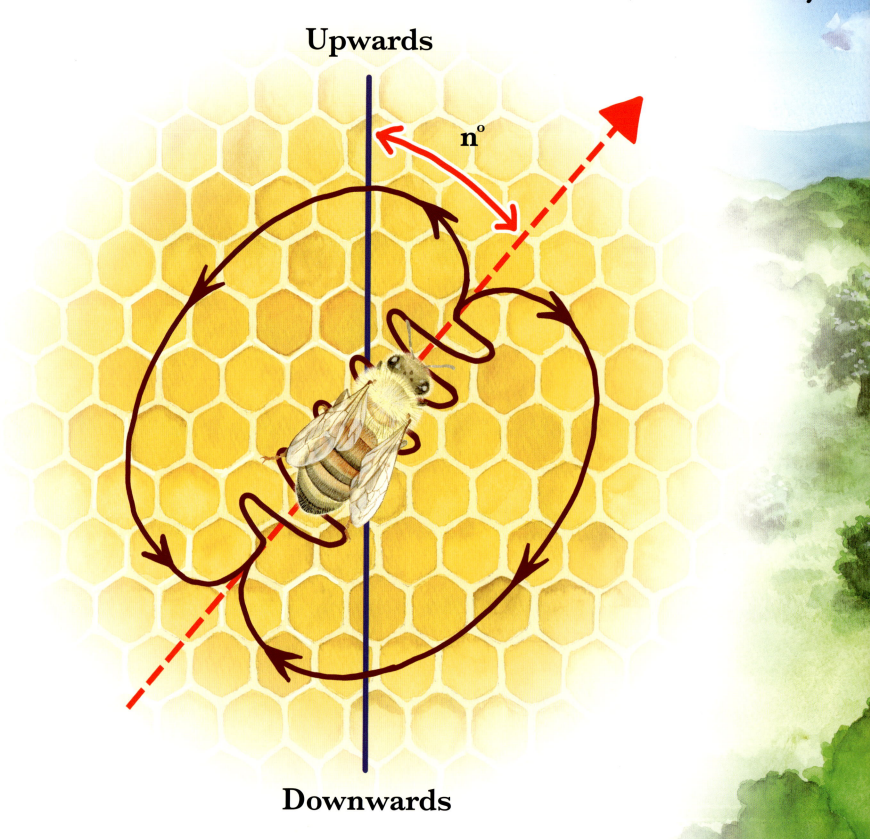

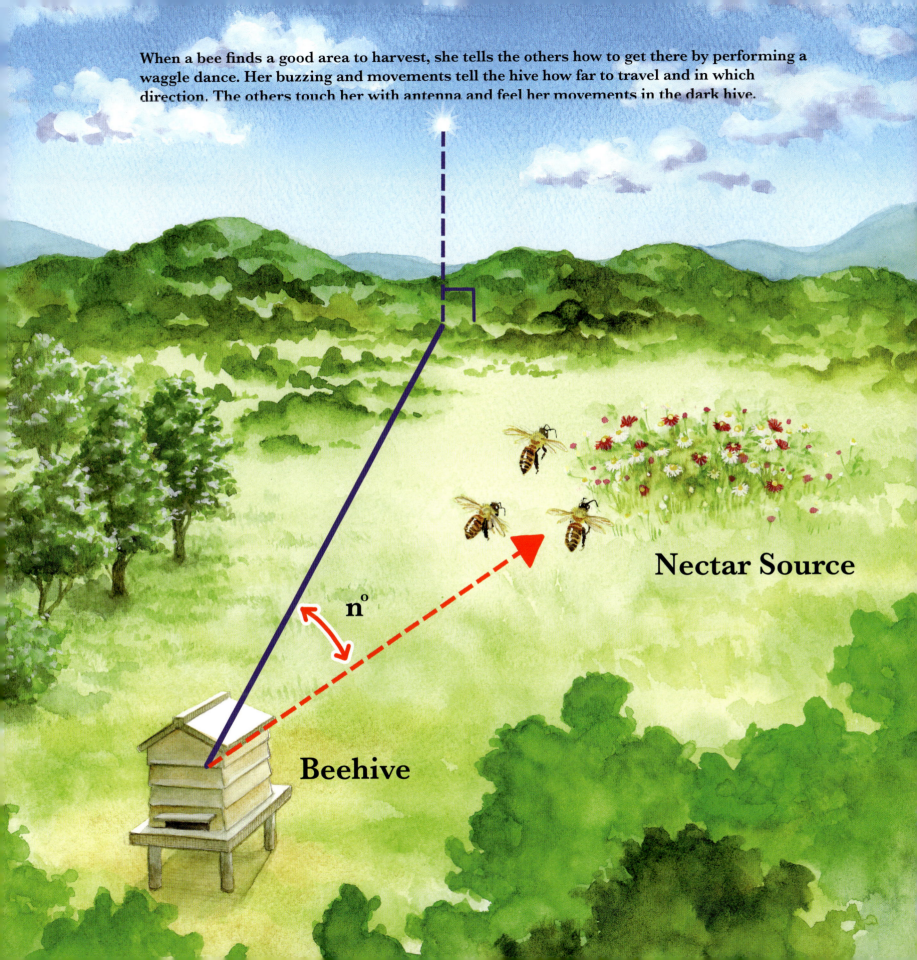

Each bee is one part of a larger whole, doing their part to keep the hive safe and healthy.

Honeybees live for the hive. They are always busy, always working. The success of the hive is their ultimate goal.

Are you ready to do your part?

"Bee Colony Life." *Arizona State University - Ask a Biologist*, 13 June 2017, askabiologist.asu.edu/bee-colony-life.

"Bee Facts." Canadian Honey Council, honeycouncil.ca/industry-overview/bee-facts/. Accessed 9 Oct. 2024.

Berthold, Emma. "What It Takes to Make a Queen Bee." *Earth and Environment*, 4 Aug. 2018, www.science.org.au/curious/earth-environment/what-it-takes-make-queen-bee.

Deep Look. "Honey Bees Make Honey ... and Bread?" *YouTube*, YouTube, www.youtube.com/watch?v=sAKkjD3nEv0. Accessed 9 Oct. 2024.

"Honey Bee Life Cycle." SCMSBA, www.scmidstatebeekeepers.org/honey-bee-life-cycle. Accessed 9 Oct. 2024.

"Honeybee." *Encyclopædia Britannica*, Encyclopædia Britannica, inc., 23 Sept. 2024, www.britannica.com/animal/honeybee.

National Geographic. "How Do Honeybees Get Their Jobs?" *YouTube*, YouTube, www.youtube.com/watch?v=9ePic3dtykk. Accessed 9 Oct. 2024.

PBS. "NOVA Bees Tales from the Hive." *YouTube*, YouTube, www.youtube.com/watch?v=I6C9th9rO0U. Accessed 9 Oct. 2024.

SciShow. "How Bees Choose Their Queen." *YouTube*, YouTube, www.youtube.com/watch?v=m_SlH3Uwslc. Accessed 9 Oct. 2024.

"The Wonder of Bees with Martha Kearney, Episode 4, Decoding the Waggle Dance." *BBC Four*, BBC, www.bbc.co.uk/programmes/p01xkyll. Accessed 9 Oct. 2024.